Fragments

Jo-Anne Patricia Cabrera

Fragments © 2022 Jo-Anne Patricia Cabrera

All rights reserved.

No part of this publication may be reproduced, stored in a retrieval system, or transmitted, in any form or by any means, electronic, mechanical, photocopying, recording or otherwise, without the prior written permission of the presenters.

Jo-Anne Patricia Cabrera asserts the moral right to be identified as author of this work.

Presentation by *BookLeaf Publishing*

Web: www.bookleafpub.com

E-mail: info@bookleafpub.com

ISBN: 9789395755337

First edition 2022

For you, who finds rest in words---

May you find a little something from here.

ACKNOWLEDGEMENT

I want to thank my parents for providing me with a life better than I could have ever imagined. Dad, I miss you and I love you. I hope we make you proud. Mom, I may not say it, but you are and will always be, my greatest Wonderwall.

To my siblings, thank you for being my first true readers. I know I can always count on you wherever life takes us.

To my lovely friends, I believe we all have met for a reason. And so, for all the laughs, tears and adventures we've shared, I thank you. You guys are beyond awesome.

To Bettina and Christine, for always being supportive and encouraging with my writing, I cannot thank you enough. Thank you for being my loyal cheer readers. Love you to bits.

PREFACE

I think I was around ten or eleven when I first stumbled upon the true beauty of poetry. I remember, I was in my cousin's place, and she had a poster up on the wall of one of her favourite poems. I was initially drawn to it, thought about it a lot and the next thing I knew, I was trying to write my own piece of poetry. Of course, not everything I did made sense, often than not, it felt like it didn't. It was like an unrequited love of sorts. But throughout the years, I find, no matter where I am or what I do, poetry has this power to comfort and serve as a reprieve. It has been a stable source of sanity for me, and it continues to.

I never thought I would be able to publish my own poetry book. I have always been insecure about my writings and didn't really feel the need to share it to the world. But I guess, the universe has a way of coercing you to do things you subconsciously want to but lack the courage to do so.

Fragments, is my first ever attempt to writing a poetry book. It took a while to get here but here we are, nevertheless. This book contains poems about relationships, finding hope and love. I wrote them in the backs of my hands, on empty paper cups, on café tissues and unwanted receipts, waiting to be kept and noticed. I tried to weave words and spun them around like threads on a needle. My hope is that it finds you, you who feel the same way about written words alike, you who say, *only poetry* can. Cheers.

Signal

I spilled my thoughts on the floor
Too tired to pick them up ---
I swallowed my dreams
Thinking the monsters were real

Courage, was alone
I bribed it to come closer
Not knowing it would escape
Just as my feet stopped
Getting colder

Maybe I am not meant
To chase the stars
When it's so damn far anyway

Maybe I need a lesson
To teach me how to let go,
And live through
My regrets

Maybe I was wrong all this time,
Who knew love
Was a traitor
And I was meant to be alone
Forever.

in bloom

there is a thunderstorm
waiting to advance and lash
its eye unto the center of your chest,

a maddening retort
slowly crawling its way out
of your unassuming solitary fort ---
a reckoning,
growing out of your bones.

this,
won't be the last
of your sunsets:

remember,
there is always light
even in the darkest of your plight.

Seafarer

It was as if
no one was watching,
I wait for you from afar.

Gathered up my courage
while my hands
have now gone numb
from the cold winter breeze

It has always been
that kind of a story;

Always waiting,
        always wanting.

Never leaving,
        never coming back.

Lune

Yesterday took
one moment from me that
I cannot possibly get back

I was trying to tell myself
that fixing us isn't really going
to make you stay -

See,
I've fumbled for years
trying to keep your words
as mine
hoping it would save
us from being broke altogether
while learning how bitter
the wind taste after the season
turns into winter.

But I cannot keep
on fighting your demons ---
letting them consume you
and tearing me apart in return

sometimes,
the sky turns

into the blackest of black
even as the Moon shines
somewhere in the night.

Circles

It was minutes to midnight,
we were aware we shouldn't
stay past our bedtime
because tomorrow is another day ---
another reckoning for those
waiting to be damned

but I wasn't ready,
you weren't either

your shallow breathing
complemented the starless sky
as your eyes reflected
of nothing but pains and regrets

You said,
goodbyes
were easiest when feelings
are but empty

It seemed nothing to you
my love,
but it was *I*
who never
really left.

The truth about the I

If only you can see through
all the skin on my body
get past all the arteries and veins
that make me up,
swim amongst the million
neurons in my brain
learn to figure out
the back door to my most disturbing,
intimate and bizarre
dreams and fantasies ---

you would appreciate
why I chose to leave
     and stay away from you
     and not bother you
     one more bit than my tiny fingers
     could have ever done.

Film out

The shadows linger longer tonight.

Stealing the show
they keep on persisting,
whispering, we're a little bit behind.

Waving signals across the nightfall
a deep pitch-black -

Somewhere,
       someone hums a tune.

Somehow,
       we know we are forgiven.

Reflections

The clock seemed
to have paused
for an eternity -

I wasn't sure
what being "here"
meant anymore

I reek of a day's old
perfume
and the cracks
on my glasses
cloud my judgment

I looked at the mirror
and saw no one
but blurred images,
contortions
of a perceived reality
which were all a stranger
to my own understanding -

I took a step forward
tried to probe further
but all I ever found

were traces of you,

still bound by gravity
forever attacking my sanity.

Belem

Goodbye, goodbye
for now,
I'll kiss you goodnight
but don't go looking for me
when the Sun touches the horizon

I will be long gone
faraway ---
where there is no more
of your memory

And none of our love
To remember.

Fader

Living through sunsets
through cracks in the walls, we witness
Long drives, to steep hikes and never-ending
conversations: on the rooftop, on your couch, on
my lap ---
on listless evenings, we thrive and try again

Strangers on every corner we meet, with smiling
hearts
we carry on

Such quiet nights and lonely days seem like our
fortune
I won't ask for a lifetime of bliss
we've wasted too much time looking for each
other:
in the rain, in the dark, in another person's heart

I keep on listening to you but I can't make you
stay
too much regret hanging in the air -
It was true then,
when I secretly wished for your happiness
as I watched you walk away...

Wallflower

The sound stops
tracks written across walls
here lie scattered books
that still smell of
second-hand stores
sketches of figures,
un d o ne -
I lay beside you
a hand under my head,
the other intertwined
comfortably against
your tiny fingers;
I let out a hum
and you returned
with a grunt
half-asleep you were,
probably
still dreaming about it all...

Rebirth

I wish to fracture
my memory of you

Maybe, this is the only way
To regrow bones and heal completely.

Amy Jade

Lie, is the truth
that your heart
can't say -

It trembles and curls
at your lips,

It curses the bond
you fail
to keep.

Leave, is where we
stand right now
when the cycle continues
to stab
like daggers
on parade.

In the end,
I am nothing
left short
of giving ---

After all,
Lie, is the game
and

Lose, is this
Motherf*cker's name.

Candlelight

Your voice is the sound
that delays my heartbeat;
your very own light,
is where I want to hide -
in your silence
I have found my home.

I know now,
I will never be alone.

A prelude

Sometimes when it's dark
I take my heart out of my chest
wash it in the rain,
stitch it back up
until it's ready to beat again.

This way,
there won't be wasted tears
running down my face
and no more sleepless nights
wondering where
your Shadows disappear.

Sarang

I hope,

I hope you find the love
That makes you go
madly curious about life.

The kind which drives you
To declare how
damn beautiful it is
To be alive --

      every.
        single.
          fucking.
            day.

Gypsy

There is that unresolved confusion
inside every one of us –
that feeble ringing in the ears,
that solitary feeling you get out
of empty rooms
and coffee cups ---
Lapses in memory:
forgetting the keys to your apartment,
where you parked your car at,
your mom's favourite cake,
your lover's birthday,
your best friend's wedding date ---
they all come together.

A conundrum,
you say to yourself.
There won't be any confessions tonight
and you know it.
One day, they will forgive.
This darkness we call
Shall soon cover for our shortfalls.
But for now, we level (even if it's all for a
show).

A revolution

There is no room
for us now
only tiny
     s p a c e s
to contain our raging hearts.

But we'll fight
'til this world
gets it right.

Eureka

There's always a story
to be written,
in the silence of the night
and in between the solitary phase
of the early morning hour.

Something that
comes out of the blue
yet so easily,
creates something
out of the void.

On Break-ups

We all hurt the same -
    the same spot,
    same organ
    always the same culprit.

Maybe, we are not that different
    for when it comes to love,
    we all can speak the same language...

El Retiro

What does it take
for you to give me back
what I've lost?

My darling,
we've all been through
dark days and heavy greys
Slept beside open books,
and empty bottles of wine
in this room that reek of cigarettes and old
perfume ---

Still, what we said remained
unheard -
what was spoken felt
like dying insults to the wound;
a fair jab to the right corner
of our unbroken silence

We never knew what was coming -
so we both left,
and never looked back.

Today, the sky turned its usual hue
while our hearts remained sad and blue.

www.ingramcontent.com/pod-product-compliance
Lightning Source LLC
Chambersburg PA
CBHW061323140726
47998CB00007B/2526